UNTROUBLED BY THE UNKNOWN

TRUSTING GOD IN EVERY MOMENT

FR. MIKE SCHMITZ

ASCENSION

West Chester, Pennsylvania

Nihil obstat: Rev. J. Brian Bransfield, STD
Censor librorum
November 1, 2021

Imprimatur: + Most Reverend Nelson J. Perez, DD
Archbishop of Philadelphia
November 8, 2021

Ascension
PO Box 1990
West Chester, PA 19380
1-800-376-0520

ascensionpress.com
Cover design: James Kegley

Printed in the United States of America
23 24 25 26 27 5 4 3 2 1

ISBN 978-1-954882-02-7 (trade book)
ISBN 978-1-954882-03-4 (e-book)

CONTENTS

THE
SUNDAY
HOMILIES
WITH
Fr. Mike Schmitz
COLLECTION

WELCOME TO **THE SUNDAY HOMILIES WITH FR. MIKE SCHMITZ COLLECTION**

Each booklet in this series has been created to invite Catholics to grow closer to God through reflections from Fr. Mike.

These booklets are short and relatable, with features that will help you apply what you read to your own life.

Quotes and Bible verses throughout the booklets will help you zero in on the key points.

Questions after each section prompt you to reflect and help you to dive deeper into the topic being presented. We recommend that you pray or journal with these questions as you make connections to your everyday life. (They also make great prompts for small group discussion, while keeping in mind that not everyone in your group may feel comfortable answering those of a more personal nature.)

Meditations are provided after each reflection to help you take the topic directly into prayer. We recommend setting aside some time after each chapter to read the meditation and pray or journal with it.

Each reflection ends with a challenge to put what you have learned into action. These challenges invite you to enter into prayer, serve others, make a resolution for the week, and more.

It is our sincere hope **The Sunday Homilies with Fr. Mike Schmitz Collection** helps you along the way in your journey toward holiness. May God bless you!

*Note: This booklet is adapted from a series of homilies given by Fr. Mike Schmitz.

CHAPTER 1

TRUSTING IN MERCY

The end of John 20 is probably one of my favorite lines in the entire Gospel of John. It says, "Jesus did many other signs in the presence of the disciples, which are not written in this book; but these are written that you may believe that Jesus is the Christ, the Son of God, and that believing you may have life in his name" (John 20:30–31). It's so personal—Jesus did many things, but these are written. Why? So that *you* might believe. St. Peter says, "Without having seen him you love him; though you do not now see him you believe in him" (1 Peter 1:8).

> "These are written that you may believe that Jesus is the Christ, the Son of God, and that believing you may have life in his name."
>
> —John 20:30–31

So many times, when we come to Mass and we're praying, it can feel impersonal. Sometimes, it can feel like God is way far away up there and holiness is for people living in other times when there's more peace and more security. But that's not true. In fact, let's talk about a woman named Helena.

"HOW LONG?"

Helena was born in Poland in 1905, a little over 100 years ago. It was a time of massive upheaval, and her family was poor. Imagine Helena's world at that time in that place. Her whole childhood was marked by World War I and the devastation that spread over all of Europe.

When she was seven years old, Helena had the very clear recognition that God was calling her to be a religious sister. But in the midst of so much uncertainty and insecurity in the world around her, she didn't act on that call. At sixteen, she had to leave home, and she became a housekeeper. She only had three years of education. Imagine being poor like Helena in the midst of this war-torn land and leaving home as a teenager to become a housekeeper.

Helena worked as a housekeeper for three years. Then, at one point she was at a party, dancing in a pink dress. In the middle of this party, she saw a vision of Jesus—and he wasn't Jesus glorified or even Jesus as he looked walking through the streets of Nazareth. This was Jesus who had been beaten and scourged. He looked up at Helena, and he asked her, "How long shall I put up with you and how long will you keep putting me off?"[1] Helena could have said, "I have a lot of good reasons, Lord. There's so much uncertainty in my life. There's so much insecurity. I have to put this off." But in that moment it was clear to Helena that despite the uncertainty and insecurity, she needed to move.

At nineteen, Helena entered a convent. You might think everyone would recognize that she's an amazing woman. But in the first months and years in the convent, the people assessing her wrote down only one comment about Helena. They wrote down three words: "No one special." She was in the convent and that was wonderful, but she was not seen as a hero. Yet it was to this woman that God would entrust the single most important message for our time.

And she almost missed it. Why? Because of all the insecurity, all the uncertainty that surrounded her life.

INSECURITY

We live in a time of insecurity right now. Things that were secure, stable, and normal are no longer stable, they're no longer secure, they're no longer normal—in big ways and in small ways. In the COVID lockdowns of 2020, even small things became unstable. We didn't have freedom to travel, we couldn't go wherever we wanted to go, and we couldn't see whoever we wanted to see.

I was talking with some older women recently who had spent their entire lives working really hard. They took a bunch of risks when it came to business and finance. They invested and saved up their money so that at the end of their lives they would have wealth that they could share with people. They wanted to do something really good with the money they saved. Now, in the midst of these uncertain times, all the savings that were the result of their lifelong work are gone. They've lost so much.

I think about all of the college athletes whose seasons were cut short in 2020. The seniors couldn't finish their last year of athletics, or if they were spring athletes, they couldn't even start—their season was taken away from them after a lifetime of hard work. If you're going to be an athlete in college, that means that you have spent your entire life directed toward your sport. You don't just happen to be an athlete in college. You have to work for it. Think about this: there was someone in the spring of 2020 who would have been crowned the best athlete in the country, who instead went unknown. Everything these athletes worked for was just gone—talk about insecurity.

Or think again of students in 2020. If you remember your time in high school or in college, you may remember your idea of how things were going to look and what you were going to do during spring semester of senior year. You probably knew you would get to do all those things you were looking forward to doing when you were a freshman. But for the seniors in 2020, that year was just gone. Students left for spring break and didn't even get to come back. They didn't get to say goodbye to their friends. They experienced insecurity.

There's also insecurity with jobs. There was so much unemployment in 2020. There's insecurity with health. So many of us are walking around wounded, and we realize the insecurity that we're surrounded by, even the death we're surrounded by. Whatever it was in which we placed our strength, whatever it was we were counting on, whatever it was that gave us our security—it's gone.

IS OUR FAITH FRAGILE?

One of the things that this insecurity reveals is that security is an illusion. Certainty is an illusion. Our plans are easily thwarted. Our strength, our talents, and our power can be real—but they run out.

Living in this world that is insecure reveals that oftentimes, our peace is passing. Too often, our faith is fragile. When we meet insecurity, our faith can be lost in a moment.

When things are "normal," we can forget that security is an illusion. But it would be incorrect to imagine that security is normal and insecurity is abnormal. As we walk through this world that is insecure, we realize that certainty and security are illusions.

So let's ask, "What if?" In the midst of an insecure world, what if we had hope that could endure? What if we had joy that could still rejoice in the midst of sorrow? What if we had a faith that wasn't fragile but was forged in the midst of adversity? What if we had a peace that surpassed all understanding, even when the future was uncertain?

WHAT THE FIRST CATHOLICS KNEW

We can ask those questions because that's what the first Catholics had. In Acts of the Apostles chapter 2, we read that they had this peace and this joy, yet they were not living in a world that was any more secure than we're living in.

> The first Catholics had peace and joy, yet they were not living in a word that was any more secure than ours.

So how did they have hope where things were hopeless? How did they have peace where things were absolutely not peaceful? How did they have a life rooted in faith when there was nothing tangible they could count on?

St. Luke says that they devoted themselves to teaching, the breaking of the bread, the prayers, and communal life. The "teaching" here means that they were connected to the bishops—the Magisterium of the Church. The "breaking of the bread" means they were connected to the Eucharist. They were devoted to prayers, too, and to the communal life that they shared with each other.

But then the Scripture goes on to say that many of them did something surprising. Many of them who had possessions and property sold their possessions, and they placed the money at the feet of the apostles. Now, what are they doing here? They're taking whatever would give them security and they're giving it away.

THE FAITH OF THE FIRST CHRISTIANS

"And they held steadfastly to the apostles' teaching and fellowship, to the breaking of the bread and to the prayers ... And they sold their possessions and goods and distributed them to all, as any had need. And day by day, attending the temple together and breaking bread in their homes, they partook of food with glad and generous hearts, praising God" (Acts 2:42, 45–47).

These three things—possessions, property, and prestige—are what you and I rely on for security. When things are going crazy around us, we open our bank accounts and think, "OK, there's more than $10 there," and that gives us peace. The first Catholics took what gives us peace and they gave it away. They took what gives us certainty and confidence and they said, "I'm going to let go of it." In the midst of overwhelming insecurity, they chose voluntary vulnerability when they gave away their possessions.

Also, they gave away property. For us, property is easy to accumulate. You can go buy a field or a house. It costs a lot of money, but you can still do it. Back in the times of the apostles, though, you couldn't just go buy property. Property was typically entrusted to you by your parents or your grandparents. It may have been given to your family when Joshua brought the children of God across the Jordan into the Promised Land, and your goal was to give that property to your great-great-great-grandchildren. Instead, these first Catholics said, "I'll let go of that property that would have given me security. I will choose voluntary vulnerability."

Finally, they let go of their prestige and what people thought of them. They said, "I'm just going to choose the Lord and follow him no matter what people are thinking." Can you imagine doing that? Can you imagine having the kind of freedom that would allow you to choose voluntary vulnerability in the midst of incredible insecurity?

I know for myself, if it "gets real," I can have some anxiety. I can feel fearful. But for the first Christians, vulnerability didn't make them afraid. In fact, Acts 2:46 gives this small detail: "they partook of food with glad and generous hearts." What would cause us fear, making us feel even more insecure, brought them joy.

So the question is this: What did they know that we don't know? Sometimes, it's easy to think that we know so much more about the world and technology than they knew back then, but we've forgotten one of the most important things. They knew what we've forgotten. They knew that security is an illusion. They knew that trials are normal and insecurity is the rule.

TESTING REVEALS, PURIFIES, AND STRENGTHENS

In fact, the first Catholics knew that insecurity is not just the rule—it's necessary. That's why St. Peter says, "Do not be surprised at the fiery ordeal which comes upon you" (1 Peter 4:12). These times of testing are not arbitrary. St. Peter says that trials are good for us. We need them.

> The first Catholics knew that insecurity is not just the rule—it's necessary.

Times of insecurity can be devastating, but they're also absolutely necessary because a time of trial or testing does at least three things. Testing reveals, it purifies, and it strengthens.

First, testing reveals. When you take a test in school, it reveals whether you knew the subject or not. It's not just a hoop to jump through before you can move to the next grade level—its purpose is to reveal whether you have learned what you were supposed to learn. Fitness tests reveal the truth about your physical reality right now. Even taking a medical test reveals something you need to know because it tells you if you have an illness. Tests reveal the truth that you need to know, even if it's painful.

Second, testing purifies. Insecurity is a test that reveals where I have placed my hope. It reveals the source of my security, and revealing the source of my security gives me the chance to change. So I might look around and realize, "Lord, so much of my security and my peace doesn't come from you." Maybe my peace comes from my bank account, or from this or that relationship. Maybe my peace comes from my health—I could go on down the list of things I look to for peace and security. Insecurity is a test that reveals what those are, and it gives me the chance to purify the source of my strength.

Finally, testing strengthens. Insecurity is a test that strengthens because I can become more rooted in Christ. If I'm given the chance to reassess the source of my strength, I can say, "Lord, now I'm going to be more rooted in you." If you and I are more rooted in Christ, we are more powerful in Christ: it gives us strength. St. Peter tells us to go through this test so that the genuineness of our faith gets purified and the authenticity of our faith can be for the Lord's praise, glory, and honor (see 1 Peter 1:6–9).

> Go through this test so that the genuineness of your faith gets purified for his praise, glory, and honor.

That's what the early Christians knew that we've forgotten: security is an illusion, and therefore, testing is necessary.

JESUS IS THE ANSWER

What else did the early Christians know that we've forgotten? I think the real question is not "What did they know?" but "*Who* did they know?" That's really the question because Jesus is the answer. These early Christians came to know that Jesus is who St. John said he is. Remember, St. John wrote, "These [words of the Gospel] are written that you may believe that Jesus is the Christ, the Son of God, and that believing you may have life in his name" (John 20:31). The early Christians heard this and knew that it is absolutely true.

> The real question is not "What did they know?"
> but "Who did they know?"

The early Christians knew the truth of Easter: Jesus Christ is God, and he conquered the grave. As God, he knows you. He has not forgotten you. He has not abandoned you. Jesus reveals the innermost secret of God, the deepest reality of God—that God is love. So in the midst of uncertainty and insecurity, the first Christians knew this profound truth of the love of God.

MERCY

There's more. God is not just love; he is the highest form of love. The Church teaches that the highest form of love is mercy. This is because mercy is the love that we don't deserve. I don't know if we ever actually deserve love, but we can say this: mercy is the love that we're given the most when we deserve it the least.

If we think about romantic love, we might be tempted to think that our good qualities attract love. That's how it is, right? A young person sees someone across a crowded room and thinks, "Wow, she's so beautiful" or

"He's so handsome." They get to know each other, and they're so funny, so charming, so witty, or they have so many other attractive qualities. Oftentimes, for other people, it is our positive traits and our strengths that draw love to us.

That might be true when it comes to people. But when it comes to mercy, it's when strength is gone that mercy is given. It's when security is gone that mercy is given. In fact, it needs to be repeated: When we deserve mercy the least is when we need it the most. And when we need it the most is when God wants to give it the most. Mercy is the love that we don't deserve, but it is the love that God most wants to give us.

> When we deserve mercy the least is when we need
> it the most. And when we need it the most is when
> God wants to give it the most.

We think it's our beauty, our strength, our security that attracts God. It is not. It is our brokenness, our weakness, our insecurity. It is our sins that attract God's love to us more than anything else.

The early Christians knew this, but we've forgotten it. They could rejoice without any external sense of security because they had an internal sense of assurance. They knew that in the midst of an incredible insecurity there is incomprehensible mercy.

✳ CONFESSION

The early Christians knew what happened on Easter Sunday when Jesus rose from the dead. The same day he rose from the dead, he came to his apostles and disciples. These were nearly all people who ran away from him and denied him, yet Jesus' first word to them was "peace." Then he breathed on them, and he said, "Receive the Holy Spirit. If you forgive the sins of any, they are forgiven; if you retain the sins of any, they are retained" (see John 20:19–23).

This is why we go to priests for confession. Can God just forgive your sins? Of course he can. But instead he gives us confession. On the first Easter, Jesus basically tells his apostles, "I forgive you. You abandoned me, you denied me, you betrayed me—but have peace. I give you my mercy; now go and bring my mercy to the world." After he gives the apostles his peace, he tells them, "As the Father has sent me, even so I send you" (John 20:21).

Why do we go to confession to priests? Because Jesus told the apostles to bring his mercy, and he gave them the ability to forgive sins. He also gave them the ability to withhold forgiveness. This is a lot of authority. It's his, but he has extended it to his priests. Why would he do this? Because he knew we would need it. Jesus isn't saying, "You're going to be perfect, but if you really need some mercy, I'll give you this little parachute here." No— he's saying, "Listen. I know your heart. I know your brokenness. I know your woundedness. I know your sins. You're going to need this, so I'm giving you this ability to be forgiven, this place you can go where you can receive my mercy. When you least deserve it is when I most want to give it."

That's why the early Christians could rejoice. They knew testing is necessary, and they knew that Jesus longs to give us his mercy. That's why, in the midst of a world that's insecure and dangerous, they could let go of the sources of their security and have glad hearts. They knew this—and we've forgotten it.

In the midst of a world that's insecure and dangerous, the early Christians could rejoice because they knew that Jesus longs to give us his mercy.

DIVINE MERCY DEVOTION

Thousands of years after the time of the early Christians, Jesus called Helena, this girl who was no one special, and entrusted to her the single most important message for our time. Through her, he reminded the world of what the first Christians knew.

In the convent, Helena took the name Sister Faustina, and Jesus continued to reveal his heart to her. She saw visions of him, which were carefully checked to confirm that they were really visions of the Lord. In these visions, Jesus said that he was entrusting Sister Faustina with a message. He wanted her to tell the world about his incomprehensible mercy.

In this war-torn world, a world of incredible insecurity, Jesus wanted Sister Faustina to tell everyone about his incomprehensible mercy. We think our sins and wounds and failures disqualify us so that when our strength is gone then hope is gone. But Jesus says that is not true. He says that what draws him to love you even more is not your strength but your weakness. It's not your wholeness, it's your brokenness. It's not your greatness, it's your sin. In fact, Jesus said to Sister Faustina that the greater the sinner, the more right he or she has to his mercy.[2]

FLOODGATES OF MERCY

This is mind-blowing. We tend to think, "I can get rid of my sources of security that are external, as long as I'm holy inside. As long as I don't fail or sin—that's my security." But Jesus tells us something different. It's not our holiness that is the source of our security—Jesus' mercy is the source of our security. He says the greater the sinner, the greater the right he or she has to his mercy. So that we understand this, he gives us a feast day that comes every year right after Easter. It's Divine Mercy Sunday.

St. John Paul II, whose life and pontificate were shaped by St. Faustina's writings, declared the first Sunday after Easter to be Divine Mercy Sunday.

On the day he proclaimed the feast, St. John Paul II is widely reported as saying, "This is the happiest day of my life." It was a day of joy because on this feast, Jesus has promised to unleash his mercy.

Why is this feast day important? There are times and places that are especially holy, and Divine Mercy Sunday is one of those times. It's a time to receive what Jesus promised to Faustina. St. John Paul II opened up Jesus' promise of mercy to the whole world on this day. John Paul II could do this as pope because he'd been given the office of binding and loosing. He said that, on this day, if any faithful person goes to confession and receives Holy Communion, it's like the moment that person was baptized: everything is erased. They are made completely whole on this day.[3]

God's mercy is so abundant that in the midst of whatever insecurity the world may bring, the floodgates of mercy are open. In the COVID lockdowns of 2020, when people couldn't get to confession and Mass on Divine Mercy Sunday because of the restrictions, there was still an opportunity to take advantage of mercy. In that year, you could make an act of contrition with the intention that you would go to confession as soon as possible. Then, you needed to make a spiritual act of communion, and the same graces were yours. Why was that allowed? Doesn't it seem like breaking the rules? No, it shows that God's mercy is abundant; God's grace is overflowing. Even in a world of insecurity, we're given incomprehensible mercy.

MERCY EVERY DAY

Divine Mercy Sunday is one day, but mercy is offered to us every day. There is a prayer of mercy called the Chaplet of Divine Mercy that I invite you to pray today and every day for the rest of your life. This prayer is basically an extension of the Mass. In the Chaplet, we pray, "For the sake of his sorrowful passion, have mercy on us and on the whole world." Jesus said that almost nothing calls down his mercy like this chaplet. He said that the souls who say this chaplet will be embraced by his mercy during their lifetime and especially at the hour of their death.

If you say, "But I'm too far gone to receive mercy; I'm too broken; I'm too hard," then listen to Jesus' words. He says, "When hardened sinners say this prayer, I will fill their souls with peace, and the hour of their death will be a happy one … When [you] say this chaplet in the presence of the dying, I will stand between My Father and the dying person, not as a just Judge but as a merciful savior."[4] In the midst of uncertainty, in the midst of insecurity and death, stands Jesus' incomprehensible mercy.

In addition to the feast day and the prayer, Jesus also gave Sister Faustina the image of Divine Mercy. Jesus said, "I promise that the soul that will venerate this image will not perish. I also promise victory over its enemies already here on earth, especially at the hour of death. I Myself will defend it as My own glory."[5]

"Jesus, I trust in you."

It's all personal, as the last words of John chapter 20 tell us: "Jesus did many other signs in the presence of the disciples, which are not written in this book; but these are written that you may believe that Jesus is the Christ, the Son of God, and that believing you may have life in his name." Jesus invites us to pray the very personal prayer that is written at the bottom of the Divine Mercy image: "Jesus, I trust in you."

ARE YOU WILLING?

Why are Divine Mercy Sunday and the Chaplet and the Divine Mercy image important? Because we realize this truth: that Jesus redeemed everyone in his life, death, and resurrection, but not everyone is saved.

There is no person who has ever lived, is living now, or will ever live for whom Jesus Christ did *not* suffer, die, and rise from the dead. He has redeemed everyone. But not all of us are saved. Why? Because not all of us are willing to accept his mercy.

This is a hard word, my brothers and sisters. If you refuse to go to confession, you're refusing his mercy. If you say, "I'll do it later," you're refusing his mercy. If you say, "Well, maybe someday. I don't know if I can let go of my sins," you're refusing his mercy.

Jesus wants to give you his mercy. The only question is this: Are you willing to let him? Make a plan of getting to confession as soon as possible. You can do this. You don't have to wait. Say yes to him now, because this world is not secure. We live in a time of great insecurity, and these words have been written down so that you might believe, and by believing you may have life in his name. Like Jesus said to Faustina, "How long will you keep putting me off?"

Jesus wants to give you his mercy. Are you willing to let him?

In a world that's broken, we have hope—because of him. In the midst of insecurity, our peace isn't passing, it is permanent—because of him. In a world of insecurity, our faith isn't fragile, it is forged like iron—because of him. And in a time of incredible insecurity, we have overwhelming trust in incomprehensible mercy. It is all because of him.

REFLECT

John 20:31 says, "But these [Scriptures] are written that you may believe." When you read the Scriptures, do you read them knowing they were written for you? How has reading the Scriptures helped you to know Jesus on a personal level?

What we're learning in life right now is that certainty is an illusion. Whatever it was that we thought gave us our security—perhaps our health, our financial stability, our jobs, our relationships, our normal day-to-day tasks—these have either been taken away or are under the threat of being taken away. What are the challenges (and maybe also the blessings) for you in learning this?

In the midst of incredible insecurity, the apostles chose voluntary vulnerability. What kind of a heart would it take for them to live that out? What are some specific character traits that you could learn from them to help you be more vulnerable and dependent on Christ?

Have you ever felt like your holiness was the source of your security? What changes now that you know that Jesus' mercy is the true source of your security?

St. Peter reminds us that trials are necessary because they reveal what we were to have learned, they purify where we have placed our hope, and they strengthen our roots in Christ. How do these three points help change your view of trials you are currently experiencing?

The apostles could rejoice without any external sense of security because they had an internal sense of assurance in God's mercy. How has Jesus assured you of his mercy through these last several weeks? What are some practical ways that you could receive more of his mercy?

PRAY

When we trust in Jesus' mercy, we have unshakeable *peace*, *faith*, and *security*. As you enter into prayer now, make it a time of appeal and surrender to the infinite mercy of Jesus.

PEACE: While there are many things that can challenge our faith, the reason for our faith is God himself. Only through a relationship with the Lord can we experience the peace that passes all understanding. For such a peace, meditate on the words, "For the sake of his sorrowful passion, have mercy on us and on the whole world."

FAITH: It is natural for us to be tempted to flee in times of trial and testing. The first letter of Peter, though, encourages us to rejoice in suffering because, like gold being refined, suffering purifies our faith. In our deepest yearning and longing for God, we rightly wish there were no impurities or impediments to our love for him. Jesus' mercy is drawn to these weakest parts, the weaknesses we feel most inclined to hide. For a faith that is forged like iron, meditate on the words, "For the sake of his sorrowful passion, have mercy on us and on the whole world."

SECURITY: In an increasingly insecure, unstable world, we can have unshakeable security by actively and repeatedly placing our trust in the mercy of Jesus. All things of this earth will pass away. All worldly support and help will ultimately fail us. As we know all too well, we will fail in our love for our Lord and others. But the merciful love of God cannot and will not ever fail us. He will not fail you. For an immovable security placed firmly in the divine mercy of our Lord, meditate on the words, "For the sake of his sorrowful passion, have mercy on us and on the whole world."

ACT ///

Today, pray the Divine Mercy Chaplet. If you haven't gone recently, make an appointment to go to confession. Let God's mercy be your security!

CHAPTER 2
AWAY FROM HOME

J. R. R. Tolkien's *The Lord of the Rings* was voted the best work of fiction in English literature not only from the twentieth century but also from the millennium.[6] You almost certainly know the story, but just in case you don't, here's the setup.

The Lord of the Rings starts in the peaceful Shire where the contented hobbits live. These hobbits are completely comfortable; they're safe; they're secure. Then, this key figure steps into their lives, and he has news. The news is that they're not as safe as they imagined. Their world, their way of life, their peace, and their very lives are insecure. The consequence is that the two main characters, the hobbits Frodo and Sam, have to leave home. In fact, they both spend almost the entirety of the rest of this story away from home. The whole novel is about these two hobbits walking through a world that is not their home—a world that is utterly insecure.

THE ROAD TO EMMAUS

Sometimes I think about those two, Frodo and Sam, when I read the Gospel about the disciples on the road to Emmaus. Remember the story? Three days after Jesus is crucified, a couple sets out on the road to the town of Emmaus. These two disciples are Cleopas and an unnamed companion. Some Scripture scholars say that it's Mary, the wife of Cleopas. If Cleopas and his wife are leaving Jerusalem to go home after the death of Jesus on Good Friday, it makes sense that they go home together.

THE ROAD TO EMMAUS

"And he said to them, 'What is this conversation which you are holding with each other as you walk?' And they stood still, looking sad ... And they said to him, 'Concerning Jesus of Nazareth, who was a prophet mighty in deed and word before God and all the people, and how our chief priests and rulers delivered him up to be condemned to death and crucified him. But we had hoped that he was the one to redeem Israel'" (Luke 24:17, 19–21).

Imagine their discussion earlier that day, three days after Jesus was crucified, talking to the other disciples and making the decision to walk away. Imagine them announcing to the other disciples, "You know, guys, we're just going to head home. We're kind of done, and we're really tired of not being home."

I think we've all had that feeling when we've been away from home for a long time. We feel like, "I just want to get back home. I want to get back to normal."

BACK TO NORMAL

Let's think about those three words, "back to normal." So often, things are turned upside down in our lives, and we just want things to get back to normal. Maybe we lost a job, and we want to go back to work. Maybe a family member got sick, and we just want to go back to our regular schedules and routines without the doctors' visits and the medical tests and the worry about the future. Maybe a friend moved away and we want to go back to where we can see that friend face-to-face and not just talk on the phone or over Zoom. During the lockdowns of 2020, a lot of us went through this. A lot of us just wanted to go out, to not have to wear a mask.

For so many of us, that's the goal—just to get back to normal. Maybe getting back to normal means that we want to go back to thinking that we can have security. But there comes a time in every one of our lives that we have to be reminded that security is an illusion and certainty is a mirage. Normal *is* insecure. Normal *is* dangerous. Normal *can* get us tired.

We can identify with Sam and Frodo, who just want to go back home to the Shire. They, and we, just want to pretend that there isn't so much death or violence in the world. We want to pretend there isn't so much evil.

Or maybe we are like Cleopas and his companion on the road to Emmaus. Since they were disciples, they let go of their sources of security on purpose when they decided to follow Jesus. But as they walked along the road to Emmaus, they probably just wanted to get back to all those things in their lives that gave them a sense of security. Those things are false sources of security, but I can imagine them talking on the way, saying, "You know what? I'll be happy when we just get home. I'll be happy when I can sleep in my own bed."

What they would be saying is this: "I'll be happy when I have this particular outcome."

OUTCOMES

We say that, too. Too often, perhaps, our sense of security is tied up with outcomes. We'll say things like, "I'll be happy when this test is over. I'll be happy when I can get a better job. I'll be happy when I can see my parents or I can see my kids. I'll be happy when … I'll be at peace when …"

Now, certain seasons of life are hard. Think of finals week for students. It's not a bad thing to say, "I'll be happy when this test is over." The problem comes when we say not just, "I'll be happy when …" but we say, "I can only be happy *if …*" or "I can only have peace *if …*" or "I can only have joy *if …*" Because as long as we need particular outcomes, joy and peace remain insecure and happiness is conditional.

My faith is always going to be fragile and my hope is always going to be destructible as long as it's based on outcomes. If I can't wait to get back to normal and that's the condition for my happiness, my life will always be insecure.

> My faith is always going to be fragile and
> my hope is always going to be destructible as
> long as it's based on outcomes.

LIVING IN EXILE

If "normal" is not the same as "secure" or "comfortable," then we have to ask a question: What does "normal" mean? What's normal for a Catholic?

In 1 Peter chapter 1, St. Peter helps us find the answer when he says, "Conduct yourselves with reverence during the time of your sojourning" (1 Peter 1:17, NAB). Actually, the word St. Peter is using is "exile." The word exile comes from a Greek word, *perokia*, which has two parts: *par,* which basically means "not," and *oikios*, which means "house" or "home." So the word "exile" comes from a Greek word that means "not home."

"Conduct yourselves reverently during the time of your sojourning."

—1 Peter 1:17, NAB

St. Peter is saying, "Conduct yourselves reverently during this time of being not home." He is reminding these Christians to remember this truth. For the Catholic, this is a life spent not home.

Since this is not home, what do we have to do? We have to live this life well; that's what St. Peter means when he says, "Conduct yourselves reverently." When I hear the word reverently, I just think of folded hands and solemnness, but that's not what St. Peter means. No—reverently means thoughtfully and intentionally. It means not carelessly.

So St. Peter is telling us not to live carelessly. He is calling us to live this life well but to remember that we are not at home and that's normal. We're called to live without conditions. Our security is not based on outcomes.

As Christians, we are called to live without saying, "Something has to change in order for me to have joy or peace or happiness." We are called to live without saying that—unless we add two more words: the words "in me." We *can* say, "Something has to change *in me* for me to have joy or to have peace." Why can this be a condition for our happiness? Because we realize we might be clinging to things that steal our peace.

If we act like we are at home in life, we can hold onto stuff that actually strips us of joy and makes it impossible for us to be close to God. There are some things that might have to change in us before we can have joy or peace. That's why St. Peter is telling us to live thoughtfully, live intentionally, and not live carelessly as we walk through the world where we are not home.

LIVING POWERFULLY

We are not home, but we can still live powerfully. Although we are walking through an insecure world, that does not mean we have to live in a way that's insecure.

As long as we have one thing, then we get to walk securely through this world where we're not home. It's the one thing that Cleopas and his companion on the road to Emmaus *don't* have. They're walking away because they don't have this.

On the road to Emmaus, Jesus joins Cleopas and his companion and asks what they're talking about. They don't recognize him, so they say, "Are you the only one who doesn't know about these things? Jesus of Nazareth, a prophet mighty in deed and word, was handed over by our chief priests and elders to be crucified" (see Luke 24:19–20). And then they say these words that reveal the condition of their hearts: "But we had hoped" (Luke 24:21). This is the past tense—these words reveal that they don't hope anymore.

They reveal in that moment that their faith is fragile, and their hope is destructible. Why? Because it is based on outcomes. They even say that it was based on an outcome: "We had hoped that he was the one to redeem Israel." They had hoped that Jesus would redeem Israel in a very specific way, and when they didn't get that outcome they wanted, they were done.

They walked away and lost hope. "We had hoped." They know they're not home and they're trying to get there, but they're walking weakly and they're walking away. They're walking alone because they don't have this one thing: hope.

I think it's really important to realize that they could have chosen hope. They go on to say, "Besides all this, some women from our group went to the tomb and the stone was rolled back, but the body they did not find. In fact, we saw a vision of angels telling us that he was alive" (see Luke 24:22–23). Other people went and verified that Jesus had risen, so it wouldn't have been unreasonable for them to trust and have hope. It wouldn't have just been a wish for them. Hope was an option.

HOPE IS NOT OPTIMISM

Let's talk about hope. We usually use the word "hope" to mean a wish. I really, really want something, so I say that I "hope" it will happen. I "hope" it's a nice day today. I "hope" that I can get my dream job someday. Those are just vague wishes, or just being optimistic.

An optimist is someone who just has this vague wish for life or this idea of positive thinking. But that's not what Christians are. In fact, optimism can kill you.

You might know the story of Admiral James Stockdale. He was a Navy Admiral and a pilot in the Vietnam War. He had flown over two hundred fighter missions before his plane was shot down in Vietnam and he was taken a prisoner. He remained a prisoner of war for one of the longest stretches that anyone was a prisoner of war in US military history. He was imprisoned for almost eight years in the Hanoi Hilton, a devastating prison camp. When Admiral Stockdale was brought to the prison camp, his bones were already fractured from his plane crash. As a high-ranking officer, he was the target of many of his captors' tortures. He was in solitary confinement for over four years, tortured almost daily, and he survived, and so did so many men with him. But many men didn't survive.

When asked in an interview who didn't make it out of those circumstances, Stockdale responded,

"Oh, that's easy. The optimists."

The interviewer was kind of puzzled by that, saying, "The optimists? I don't understand."

And Stockdale continued, "The optimists. Oh, they were the ones who said, 'We're going to be out by Christmas.' And Christmas would come, and Christmas would go. Then they'd say, 'We're going to be out by Easter.' And Easter would come, and Easter would go. And then Thanksgiving, and then it would be Christmas again. And they died of a broken heart."[7]

Optimism is not hope. The optimism of those men who didn't survive was based on outcomes, but hope is not based on outcomes. Hope is not positivity, and it's not based on positivity.

Hope is based on a person. That's why St. Peter says, "Your faith and hope are in God" (1 Peter 1:21). We are called to have faith and hope not in outcomes but in God. In fact, we can think of the words of King David, who says, "I keep the LORD always before me; because he is at my right hand, I shall not be moved" (Psalm 16:8). The Lord ever will be at my right hand. He's with me, and therefore I shall dwell in hope again. Our hope means that we dwell with the Lord. Our hope is not based on positivity; it's based on a person.

> "I keep the LORD always before me; because he is at my right hand, I shall not be moved."
> —Psalm 16:8

TRUST IN JESUS

I like to define hope this way: hope is trust in another extended into the future. Hope is when you know a person is trustworthy now and you know they're going to be trustworthy in the future.

Our hope is trust in Jesus extended into the future. Hope is not a wish that things will change, but it's trust in the One who will never change. We're walking through this world of insecurity, and we're not home, but we trust Jesus now and for the future. Like David, we know Jesus walks with us and so we dwell with hope.

> Hope is not a wish that things will change,
> but it's trust in the One who will never change.

I love what Jesus does next on the road to Emmaus: he opens up the scriptures to Cleopas and his companion. He shows them everything in the Bible that was about him. I think one of the reasons he does that is to help them remember.

When you remember where God was, it reveals where he is. Looking back in the Scriptures, we can remember what he has done. That's important, because when you remember what he's done, it reveals what he's doing. Jesus says to remember who he is. When you remember who he is, it reveals that he does not change. He's saying, "Remember what I've done. I've been faithful. So you don't walk alone. Remember where I was? Well, here I am now—and you don't walk alone. Remember who I was? Well, I do not change, and I am with you now. You're not home, but you do not walk alone."

WALKING ONWARD

We are not alone. This is one of the reasons why those who hope are the ones who act. Hope is a virtue that moves. Hope is a virtue that acts and guides. If I only have wishful thinking or optimism, I'll say, "I'll sit back and wait. Hopefully things will get better." But true hope is the virtue that guides our feet to move, because hope states that acting matters. The *how* you live matters. And it matters, no matter the outcome.

Why is acting important? Because I trust Jesus and I know I do not walk alone even when all seems lost.

As Frodo and Sam are walking through their dangerous world in *The Lord of the Rings*, far from home, they reach a moment when it seems that all is lost. It's a devastating scene in the book and in the movie. Frodo, who is the ring bearer, is absolutely beaten down, tired of being not home, and he looks at Sam, who is his helper. It's a kind of Simon of Cyrene moment, when Simon helps Jesus carry his cross. Frodo says, "I can't do this, Sam." Sam is supposed to be the source of encouragement, but he looks at Frodo and says, "I know." He doesn't argue or say everything is fine. He says, "I know it's all wrong. We shouldn't even be here."

You might feel like that. Maybe you don't feel it now, but maybe you have felt it in those great moments of grief in your life when you just want to get back to normal—back to the time before you got sick, or before you lost your job, or before those people walked away. In those great moments of grief, just hear Sam saying, "I know. We shouldn't even be here."

But Sam goes on to say,

> It's like in the great stories, Mr. Frodo. The ones that really mattered. Full of darkness and danger, they were. And sometimes you didn't want to know the end. Because how could the end be happy? How could the world go back to the way it was when so much bad had happened? But

in the end, it's only a passing thing, this shadow. Even darkness must pass. A new day will come. And when the sun shines it will shine out the clearer. Those were the stories that stayed with you. That meant something, even if you were too small to understand why. But I think, Mr. Frodo, I do understand. I know now. Folk in those stories had lots of chances of turning back, only they didn't. They kept going. Because they were holding on to something.[8]

And then defeated Frodo says, "What are we holding on to, Sam?" Sam looks at his friend and he says, "That there's some good in this world, Mr. Frodo, and it's worth fighting for." Hope is not lost.

Even when we're not home, hope is the virtue that moves us to keep walking, to keep fighting. J. R. R. Tolkien, the author of *The Lord of the Rings*, was a Catholic man, and he said *The Lord of the Rings* is a Catholic book. Even though he didn't put it in this scene, Tolkien knew the good has a name.

There is some good in this world, and it's worth fighting for. The name of this good is Jesus. He is the one who has entered into suffering and death, who left his home to be with us so we wouldn't walk alone.

WHEN HOPE ENDS

We trust in Jesus, trusting that he's here now and he will be there at the end. There's going to come a moment in each of our lives when hope is no longer an option. If we have chosen to say yes to him, and if we have remained steadfast in our commitment to that choice, it will be the greatest moment.

We have hope until the end, and then in the end, if we have chosen him, hope will no longer be necessary. In that moment when we see him face-to-face, and for all eternity, we won't have hope because we'll have *him*. We won't have hope because he'll have *us* in heaven forever. And after all this insecurity, after all this experience of being not home, after all this walking and living and moving, there comes the time when hope is gone and all that's left is *him*. And then we can rest—because then, we will be secure.

REFLECT

Our security can often be tied up in outcomes. Have you found that there are times when your security, happiness, or peace is conditional? Have there been times when it isn't?

St. Peter says that since we live "not home" as Christians, we must live reverently (or "not carelessly"). What is one way that you know you are called to live more intentionally or thoughtfully?

What do you think it means to say that hope is dwelling with the Lord? How does this apply to your life?

Have you ever had to trust someone with something important? What was that experience like? How is putting your trust in Jesus similar or different?

Christian hope isn't optimism; it is trust in Another extended into the future. Is your hope connected with the Person of Jesus or do you place your trust in something else?

Jesus opened the Scriptures so the disciples would know where he has been and realize where he *is*. Based on where God has been in your life in the past, where can you find him now in the present? Based on who he has been, who do you know him to be now?

The day will come when we will no longer hold onto hope because we will hold onto him. Do you think about that day? Do you pray for it?

PRAY

As we have seen in this chapter, "Hope is *trust* in *another* extended into the *future*." We are not home yet. By God's grace, someday we will be. It is in this foreign land that we now enter into prayer with Jesus.

"Hope is *trust* ..." Though this world is not our home, it can seem like it is. The busyness of everyday life can convince us that what we see is all that is. To counter this illusion, we must entrust our lives to God's care each day, placing our earthly, passing cares into his heavenly, eternal hands. Do this as you begin your time of prayer now.

"... in *another* ..." Remember that you are not placing your life into the hands of another human being. You are not trusting in another; you are actively trusting in *the Other*, the One by whom the universe was created and is sustained. You are actively choosing to rely on the God of all things.

"... extended into the *future*." Finally, endeavor to "pray without ceasing" (1 Thessalonians 5:17). When you have begun this prayer of hope and trust, make it an intention never to stop. Since God never changes, this prayer never needs to have a final "amen."

ACT ///

This week, keep your focus on God's faithfulness and your trust in him. If you find yourself placing your security in anything other than him, surrender that to him and ask him to be your security.

CHAPTER 3
FACING THE UNKNOWN

During the lockdowns of 2020, there were so many things we wanted to know. We said things like "I just want to know when this is going to end. I just want to know when I can get back to work. I just want to know whether students are going to have graduation. I just want to know when I can see people in person again."

I have a niece who was supposed to have her First Holy Communion in the spring of 2020. When it was postponed, I wanted to know when it was going to happen. I have a nephew who was supposed to be confirmed in the spring of 2020. I wanted to know when it would happen. A lot of us had questions like this.

I JUST WANT TO KNOW

Whenever there is uncertainty, we just want to know. When will the things happen that are supposed to happen? When can things be normal? These questions can be summarized by those words: I just want to know.

I think the reason we want to know is this: we think that if we know, we don't have to worry. Here's a little truth: you *don't* have to worry. Not worrying is actually an option. But so many of us walk around with anxiety and worry that can dominate our lives, to a normal level or even to a clinical level.

Recently more students around the country have sought mental health help for issues of anxiety than for issues of depression. Anxiety is on the rise. Now, on one hand, that statistic is really good because it means that more people are asking for help. It is great that we have doctors for our minds, and the fact that people are unafraid to ask for help when they have a mental health issue is very good. And yet it's troubling that more and more people are experiencing these high levels of anxiety.

A number of years ago, I read a definition of anxiety that I thought was really helpful. According to this definition, anxiety is the overestimation of danger and the underestimation of one's ability to cope with that danger. It is true that the world is dangerous, but in so many ways our anxiety comes from wanting to know what's going to happen and wondering if we'll be able to face it. We think that if we know, then we can relax. We think that then we'll stop overestimating the danger and underestimating our ability to cope. We can be secure.

So many of us act on this idea that if we know, we can be secure. But it is a myth that knowing equals security.

WHEN WE NEED TO KNOW

Now, here's a quick caveat. Sometimes, it's very important to know. It's good to ask questions and find out the answers, because we need to know some things in order to plan or prepare or participate.

For example, a couple needs to know how many people are coming to their wedding. Why? Because they need to plan to feed their guests. So we need to know some things in order to plan. We also need to know some things in order to prepare. If you're a student, you need to know if your class is going to have an exam or not, because you need to prepare. If you're an elite athlete, you need to know whether you're going to have a championship in August or not, because your training is very tailored toward that moment.

We also need to know some things so we can participate. For instance, we need to be informed about what's going on in the country. We don't need to go to an extreme that lets the news become a constant distraction from our daily lives. But we must be aware of what is going on in our country, because we're not just residents, we're citizens.

So knowing can be very good and necessary when I need to plan or prepare or participate. But I don't need to know in order to have peace.

> I need to know in order to plan or prepare or participate. But I don't need to know in order to have peace.

FACING THE UNKNOWN

I can have peace even when I don't know what will happen. This world is insecure, yet as Catholic Christians, we are called to live without stress even when we are without security. I would say the call for Catholic Christians today is to be untroubled by the unknown.

How is that possible? How can we be comfortable with being uncomfortable? In order to be that kind of person, we need to be courageous, and we need to be confident.

To be untroubled by the unknown, we need to be courageous,
and we need to be confident.

There's a psychologist out of Canada who talks about parenting. As parents, one of your most important jobs is to protect your kids from this dangerous world, but then at some point you need to prepare them to go into the danger of this world. You can't make the world more secure, but you can help your children become courageous. After protection, that's your main job as parents. You can't make the world safer, but you can make your child stronger.

God is our Father, and God is a good parent. So God does the same thing for us. He made this world that's good but not unbreakable, and it has broken. Since it is insecure, God sends us out into this world and says, "OK, I'm not going to make it any safer, but I'm going to make you stronger. I'm going to call you to be courageous."

THE COURAGE OF MARY

We have many examples throughout the Bible of people who were courageous and untroubled by the unknown. One of the best examples is our mother, Mary. Luke 1 tells us what happens when the archangel Gabriel tells her that she is going to be the mother of the Messiah. Mary asks a clarifying question. She knew how a child would be conceived ordinarily, but scholars say that Mary and Joseph were planning on being celibate for their entire marital relationship. So Mary asks, "How is this going to happen to me if I don't have any relations with a man?" We can ask questions like "How is this going to happen?"

Gabriel gives her the answer: "The Holy Spirit will come upon you, and the power of the Most High will overshadow you" (Luke 1:35). So she says, "Behold, I am the handmaid of the Lord; let it be [done] to me according to your word" (Luke 1:38). Now imagine the courage of Mary in that moment. Imagine how untroubled she is by the unknown.

I think about how I would respond. I would be like, "But what's going to happen after that?" If I were Mary, I would want Gabriel to say, "Here's what's going to happen. Joseph's going to decide to step aside, but don't worry. I'll appear to him in a dream, and it'll be OK. Then, you're going to have to go to Bethlehem for the census, but don't worry. There will be a cave for the baby to be born, and it'll be OK. And then Herod the king is going to try to kill your son, but don't worry. I'll appear to Joseph in a dream and tell him to go to Egypt. It'll be OK. You're going to lose Jesus in the Temple for three days, but don't worry about it. After three days, he'll be there. It'll be OK."

I would want the assurance and the certainty. I would want to know what's going to happen. But Mary is not given any of that. She is just told, "The power of the Most High will overshadow you." She's just told what she needs to know now. And that's enough for her. She is untroubled by the unknown because she's courageous and confident.

THE CONFIDENCE OF MARY

Mary knows that she can be courageous because she's confident in God, not in herself. In fact, the word "confident" is from the Latin word *confidere*, which means "trust." It doesn't mean trusting in oneself but rather trusting in another.

> Mary knows she can be courageous
> because she's confident in God.

Being a phenomenal Jewish woman, Mary knows the story of Israel and the Exodus when God delivers his people from slavery in Egypt. After he leads them through the Red Sea, Scripture says, his presence was with them in a pillar of fire at night and a column of cloud during the day. When the pillar of fire or the column of cloud stopped, the people would stop. Then, when it was time to move, the fire or cloud would move, and the people would simply follow it (see Exodus 13:21–22). Imagine the confidence the people could have. They could see that pillar of fire at night and that column of cloud every single day. They could see that God was present.

I wish I could say that would be enough for me, but it wouldn't be. If I were there during the Exodus, I'd be like, "OK, when are we going to move next?" The people around me would probably be like, "Don't worry, dude. God's with you." But I would want to know where he was leading us and what was going to happen next. I would want to know. Why? Because I'm one of those believers in the myth that knowing equals security.

LETTING HIM LEAD

I just want to know where we're going to go, but God didn't tell us that. Instead, he tells us that he is with us and that he is going to lead us. Isn't that enough? Isn't that all we need to know so that we can be courageous and be confident? When it's time to stop, he'll stop. When it's time to go, he'll lead us. In the Gospel, Jesus says, "I am the Good Shepherd … My sheep hear my voice, and I know them, and they follow me" (John 10:14, 27).

> "I am the Good Shepherd … My sheep hear my voice, and I know them, and they follow me."
> —John 10:14, 27

But I'm the stupidest kind of sheep. Jesus is like, "We're going to be fine. Just follow me." But I'm like, "Yeah, where are we going? Sure, sure, I trust you and I'm going to follow you, but just tell me what's going to happen." Yet even if Jesus told me, I'd come back with more questions. Why? Because, again, I think that knowing equals security. Jesus knows I believe this myth, and he knows many of us believe it. We need to trust him instead.

Jesus is so good. Because we need to trust him, he says that the sheep don't know where he's going to lead them, but they know him. They don't know where his voice is going to lead them, but his sheep know his voice, and they follow him.

Basically, Jesus is saying to the Christian disciple, "You're not going to know where I will lead you. You don't get to know, but you do know who it is that's leading you."

HEARING GOD'S VOICE

I was talking to a college campus missionary recently about God's voice. Coming into prayer sometimes, we ask God the question, "I know I need to hear your voice, but I don't hear it. What does your voice sound like?" And finally the Lord reminded this campus missionary in prayer that he did actually write a book: the Bible. You can hear what God's voice sounds like—just take up Scripture and read. Jesus also founded a Church. Over the last two thousand years, he gave the world the Catholic Church, which speaks with his voice. Jesus said that when people hear the Church, they hear him. God gave us his voice in Scripture, and God has given us his voice through the Church.

God gave us his voice in Scripture, and
God has given us his voice through the Church.

God has spoken enough for us to know his voice. And he has spoken enough for us to know what to do right now. Here's the truth: you and I know exactly enough to act now. I might not know what's next, but I do know what's now. I am called to be untroubled by the unknown, because what's known is enough.

In the Acts of the Apostles, Peter gets up and preaches, and he cuts the people to the heart with the truth. They say, "What shall we do?" (Acts 2:37). No doubt they wanted to know what would happen next. But Peter says, "Repent, and be baptized" (Acts 2:38). He doesn't tell them what will happen next. Essentially, he tells them, "We don't know what's going to happen later, but we don't need to know that."

LIVING WISELY

So often I want to know what's going to happen because I want to make the perfect decision. I don't want to mess up or fail. News flash: we will often make the wrong decision. We will often fail. But that is not the end. When we make the wrong decision and fail, God keeps speaking.

You and I know enough to live wisely, even if not perfectly. We can ask about what we need to do now, and we can act.

There was a young man I knew who graduated from school and discerned that God was calling him to the seminary. A lot of prayer and a lot of spiritual direction went into his discernment. So he went to seminary, but after a while it was pretty clear that he wasn't called to stay in the seminary. After prayer and discernment and spiritual direction, he left the seminary to date this girl that he really liked. She liked him back, so they dated for a long time. He thought, "I've found my vocation." And then she broke up with him.

He thought, "God, what is going on? I thought this was what you wanted, but now I don't know what to do. Should I go back to the seminary? Should I date someone else? Should I stay single? God, what do you want? I just want to know, and I don't have any idea."

Then this young man came to a conclusion. He realized, "Wait a second. I don't know whether God's calling me to be a priest or to be married or to be single. But wherever he's calling me, I know the kind of person he needs me to be when I get there. If he's calling me to be a priest, then he needs me to show up there as a virtuous man. If he's calling me to be a husband and a father, he needs me to show up there as a virtuous man. If he's calling me to be single, then he needs me to show up there as a virtuous man. This means that I know enough to know what to do now."

> Wherever God is calling me, I know the kind of person he needs me to be when I get there.

The truth is that you and I know enough to act well and to live wisely now. We know enough to be courageous in the midst of insecurity and to be confident in the Lord's voice. We know enough to wait when the Lord is silent and then to move boldly when he speaks. It takes courage and confidence, but we know enough.

> We know enough to be courageous in the midst of insecurity and to be confident in the Lord's voice.

Above all, we know enough to be untroubled by the unknown. We may not know where he is leading us, but we know who is doing the leading.

REFLECT

As Christians, we are called to have peace in an incredibly insecure world. How do you think this is possible? What might this look like for you?

Have you ever wanted continual assurance every step of the way from God? What will it be like to place your security in him instead of the answers or assurance he gives?

God can speak to us in many ways, including through the Church, through Scripture, and in prayer. Have you heard God's voice before in any of these ways? If so, what was that like? If not, pick up your Bible and read God's words!

Do you worry about making the wrong decision? Has there been a time in your life when you felt that you made the wrong decision but God worked everything out in the end?

Do you have the confidence and courage a Christian needs to be secure in an insecure world? How can you build up that confidence and courage?

What are the kinds of things you find yourself worrying about? Why those things? (If you rarely worry, why do you think it is that you do not have anxiety?)

We need courage to face an insecure and dangerous world. Do you think that people can grow in courage? What kinds of things increase courage?

To live with confidence is to live "with faith" in another. Where in your life is it most difficult to "have faith" in where God is leading you?

PRAY

Most of our lives are made up of the unknown. The limited number of things each of us knows is laughable compared to those we don't. Each of us knows a few areas well, while knowing very little about other areas. For example, you might know a lot about sports but nothing about accounting. But none of us knows the future. Therefore, it can seem that we have nothing to rely on. Enter your time of prayer now with two points in mind, though.

First, what you know is enough. God knows what you *need* to know at this moment. Don't get distracted by the question marks about things you don't know, especially the future. In prayer, ask the Lord to show you the actual wealth of knowledge he has already given you.

Second, remember who is doing the leading—God. As a saying goes, "I may not know what the future holds, but I know *who* holds the future." In prayer, you are in a conversation with the Lord, your Creator and Savior! You don't need to know even one second of the future if you know him. If Jesus is with you—and he *is*—then the future is safely and securely in his hands.

ACT ///

To hear God's voice and place your security in him, you need to spend time with him. Set aside fifteen minutes for prayer each day this week. Ask God to speak to you and be your security.

CHAPTER 4
THE PLAN AND THE WAY

When my mom was a kid, she wanted to be a missionary. She heard about an organization that is now called Mercy Ships. Back then, it was a mission for medical personnel who would travel on ships and do medical missions all over the world. My mom had heard the call of Jesus in Matthew 25:35–36 where he says, "I was hungry and you gave me food, I was thirsty and you gave me drink … I was naked and you clothed me, I was sick and you visited me, I was in prison and you came to me."

My mom said, "I want to be a missionary to serve those people who are hungry and thirsty and naked and sick." She wanted to do what Jesus asked her to do. So she went to nursing school, and then she met my dad. She became a nurse and paid my dad's way through medical school, and she worked for him and she served the family … and she never went on mission.

I guess she would say that she couldn't go on mission because she was too busy being a mom. She had a plan, but it never worked out. I imagine many moms understand that. You have plans and dreams, and then the plan goes to the side because you're too busy being a mom. We'll come back to that.

PLANS

Most of us have plans. If you went to college, think of your plan when you decided where to apply. Maybe you had a plan for your major and for what job you would have after you graduated. I read a statistic recently that only 27 percent of college graduates actually get a job in a field related to their major.[9] After all that planning, investment, and time taking classes in their major, they could say, "I had a plan, and it didn't work out."

The day you graduate from high school or college is one of those transition times when you can feel really clearly that life is insecure. Many students have had a plan up to that point and have based their entire lives on their plan. And they realize that taking the next step beyond school is a step into uncertainty and insecurity.

In fact, choosing the next step after school may be the first truly insecure step that some people have ever taken. If you experienced a lot of stress over this next step, or you are a student and are experiencing a lot of stress now, that makes sense. Up to graduation, you were on track. When you were little, you went to kindergarten, and then the next step was first grade. They actually number the steps for you: first grade, second grade, third grade, and so on.

The next step for a student into high school might be stressful—now you have some choices, you have electives you can take—but still it's just going into the next numbered grade. If you go to college, you have to choose things again, and it's stressful, but there's a track to follow.

Then, when you're done with school, you have to come face-to-face with the reality that life is uncertain. The track you've been following comes to an end. Everything ahead is uncertain. It's all insecure.

Sometimes, in moments of insecurity like the moment of graduation from school, we look back and realize that we don't have the hope we thought we had. Sometimes we think we had courage and confidence, but it was actually courage and confidence in our plan. And when the plan comes to an end, we don't know what to do next.

THINKING AHEAD
WITHOUT SEEING AHEAD

Now, here's a caveat—it is good to plan. As we mentioned before, we need to prepare for the future. That's called forethought. We need to think about the future and the plan, and we need to ask, "God, where is it you want me to go?"

We need to have forethought. But no matter how much we think ahead—no matter how much forethought we have—we cannot see ahead into the future. Planning is good, but when reality hits you hard, then you have to ask, "What do I do now?"

> We need to think ahead about the future,
> but we cannot see ahead into the future.

There's something called the fog of war. In the midst of battle, there are many variables that generals and soldiers had no idea would be there and that they have no control over. When it came to preparing for battle, Dwight Eisenhower would say, "Plans are useless, but planning is indispensable."

If you go into battle without a strategy, you don't have much chance of winning. Planning is indispensable. We need to have a plan so we can make the appropriate preparations. We need to take into account all possible misfortunes so we are ready to respond to them. A Prussian general back in the early nineteenth century named Carl von Clausewitz said, "We must, therefore, be confident that the general measures we have adopted will produce the results we expect."[10] We need a plan.

Planning, engaging, and having forethought—thinking about the future— are indispensable. Yet, in the midst of all the strategy, there's so much uncertainty and insecurity. You might have a great plan, but in a war someone actually wants to defeat you. Someone wants to mess up your plan.

But you have to move forward.

After planning, we have to be ready for insecurity. Clausewitz said, "Then we must boldly advance into the shadows of uncertainty."[11] After all the forethought, we have to walk into insecurity. And that can be very painful.

WHEN THE PLAN FAILS

I remember talking with a man who contacted me because he had discerned that God had called him to a particular ministry in the Church. In order to work in this ministry, he had to leave his home and friends and move across the country. He thought it was a good plan, he thought it was God's will, and he thought it was super selfless of him to leave everything and pursue the Lord—and nothing worked out the way he wanted or planned. Basically, it all went wrong, and he asked me, "Was that the wrong decision?"

Just because the original plan failed doesn't mean taking that step was the wrong decision. It's so important for us to realize that. This is true for every one of us. Maybe the place where you thought God was going to plant you was just a place where he was bringing you to purify you. Perhaps that was actually the place he was bringing you to prepare you for the next step.

Our plans fail, but God has a plan that does not fail. When we take a step in faith, we are signing up for God's plan. If our plan doesn't work out, perhaps God is saying, "Here is this other place where I want you."

> Our plans fail, but God has a plan that does not fail.

STEPHEN

A man named Stephen was one of the first deacons of the early Church. Acts chapter 6 tells his story. The apostles realize there's so much to do in the early Church, that they need help. They not only need to preach the Word but they also need to bring food to people. So the apostles select seven men and say, "We will consecrate you to serve these poor people while we go preach." Stephen and the other deacons were ordained to be servants of God.

ST. STEPHEN, DEACON AND MARTYR

"But he, full of the Holy Spirit, gazed into heaven and saw the glory of God, and Jesus standing at the right hand of God; and he said, 'Behold, I see the heavens opened, and the Son of man standing at the right hand of God'" (Acts 7:55–56).

Imagine Stephen discerning this call to be a deacon. And the very next time we see Stephen, he's in the Temple preaching. He's proclaiming the Word. In fact, all of Acts chapter 7 describes Stephen preaching the Word. I can imagine that Stephen might have wondered why he found himself needing to preach. Stephen might have said, "I was not called to preach the Word. I was ordained for a specific purpose. I was ordained to serve."

Serving is a good thing. That's what Jesus did at the Last Supper. Stephen must have heard the stories of how Jesus at the Last Supper took off his outer garments, got down on his knees, and washed the disciples' feet. Jesus said, "I did not come to be served, but to serve" (see Matthew 20:28). So perhaps Stephen thought, "I'm not here to teach; I'm here simply to serve." And the apostles and the Lord are like, "OK, you were planning to serve, but actually you're called to preach. You didn't discern wrongly and you didn't decide incorrectly. You thought God would plant you where you would serve; he was simply preparing you to preach."

We know that preaching led Stephen to be martyred. That wasn't the plan. I'm guessing that when the apostles asked Stephen if he would be willing to help feed the hungry, he was probably not expecting it to lead to his death. But just because the original plan changed does not mean that it was wrong. And just because you discerned does not mean that you're done.

FR. WALTER CISZEK

Just because you discerned and decided on a plan does not mean you're done discerning and deciding, because following Christ is not about having a plan. Life with Christ is not about living out our plan on our own terms. It's about the process of becoming the person Christ calls us to be.

One of my heroes is a man named Fr. Walter Ciszek.[12] Fr. Ciszek was a normal guy in the early part of the 1900s here in the United States. He went to school; he played football. At one point, though, he recognized God's call to be a priest, and he responded with courage and went to seminary. This was his plan, to be a priest in his local diocese here in the United States.

FR. WALTER CISZEK
1904–1984
American priest, educated in Michigan
Missionary to communist Russia
Imprisoned in Siberia
Wrote his story in the books *With God in Russia* and *He Leadeth Me*

Then the Holy Father, the pope, said, "We need priests who are willing to be missionary priests to communist Russia." At the time, Russia was under an atheist and communistic regime. And so Fr. Ciszek said, "OK, that's what I'll do." He got all the training he needed because his plan now was to get into Russia and bring the Gospel there.

So he was ordained and sent to Poland. He had to try to find a way into Russia from Poland, but he couldn't get past the guards and the security. Then Russia invaded Poland, so he realized, "OK, I'm kind of in Russia now. Now is when I can live out this plan." But after two weeks of being an undercover missionary in communist-occupied Poland, he got captured.

Here was Fr. Ciszek's plan when he was captured: "If I'm captured, I will be faithful to the Lord. I will be unbreakable, and they will never be able to strip my faith away from me." But after a year of solitary confinement, being interrogated by those Russian agents every single day, Fr. Ciszek was broken. He describes in his book *He Leadeth Me* how they led him to an interrogation room and put documents in front of him that would disavow the United States government, and he signed them. He was so broken, they put documents in front of him that disavowed the Vatican, and he signed them. They put documents in front of him that disavowed the Church, and he signed them. Finally, they put documents in front of him that disavowed Jesus, and he signed them.

Then, when he had signed everything they put in front of him, they left him in his cell by himself with nothing but his embarrassment and failure, his guilt and shame. Then they finally sent him to a Soviet gulag in Siberia. Fr. Ciszek must have thought, "Not only did my plan not work out, but look at me; I can't even be a missionary. My plan was to go to the Russian people and bring them Jesus. Here I am, in a Soviet gulag." But then he realized that there in the gulag he was surrounded by Russian people in need of Jesus.

Fr. Ciszek was in the midst of his failure, in the midst of knowing that his plan was not reality, when he realized that he had a decision to make. He could look at this situation in two ways: either he was abandoned there, or he was led there. Either this was the thwarting of his plan, or this was actually the way that Jesus wanted him to live, the way he wanted him to walk. This was actually part of his plan.

Fr. Ciszek chose to look at his imprisonment as part of Jesus' plan, and he was able to minister to the people around him for decades. God's plan did not fail even though Fr. Ciszek's plan failed again and again.

FACING FAILURE

When we're faced with failure, we can respond with resentment or recognition. We either can have resentment and anger that our plan has been taken away and thwarted—or we can have recognition that God is here even in the midst of insecurity.

We all know people who become resentful when their plans are thwarted. They become bitter. They become small. I came across a quote that said,

"No plan survives first contact with the enemy." Another way to say it is that no plan survives first contact with reality. I had my dream, my vision, my plan—but plans fail. What matters is how quickly the leader is able to adapt, to get past that disappointment, and to get through the resentment.

When our plans fail, we are called to let go of the resentment and to recognize that God is here even in insecurity. The Christian life is not a call just to discern and be done, but it is a call to keep discerning, to keep deciding, and to keep being willing to adapt. Every one of us has to cultivate a willingness and ability to let go of our plans when God makes it very clear, through the reality we face, that that's the next good step we need to take.

> When our plans fail, we are called to let go
> of the resentment and to recognize that God
> is here even in insecurity.

We can be willing to adapt to the reality of insecurity because we realize this life is full of change. To be alive is to change. That means that to take a step is always going to be to take a risk. To be a follower of Christ is to be willing to keep taking those risks and to keep discerning.

GETTING THROUGH HEARTBREAK

This can be very difficult, so I want to pause on this topic. Recognizing God's presence in insecurity means we need to be able to get through heartbreak—through the plan-altering and dream-crushing and heart-destroying moments. We'll talk about how to get through them in a moment. But first, let's talk about timing.

We don't have to rush through seasons of heartbreak. It's not a race. Those things are real. Maybe you find yourself right now trapped in insecurity in a job you didn't plan on. Or maybe you're looking at your life right now saying, "Did I waste everything?" There's grief that comes along with those reflections. We have to get through that, but it takes time.

Maybe there are relationships you look back on, even the primary relationship in your life, where you could say, "I messed that up. I made decisions that destroyed my marriage, or my relationship with my parents, or my relationship with my kids—I did that." Or maybe it was a situation where a person walked away who had promised you his or her entire life—and that person messed up the plan. We have to learn how to get through that kind of thing, but it takes time.

Let's talk about mothers again. Too many of you know that being a mom is all about giving up; it is all about risk. You risk your heart every day once you become a parent. Since you know the insecurity and the uncertainty of life, you realize that your children—these people who have given you your greatest joy and hope—could give you your greatest heartbreak.

Too many of you moms know exactly what it's like to have your kids be taken away too soon. You mourn not just the loss of the plan, but more than that you mourn the loss of this person who was made from you.

Sometimes, even worse, there's another kind of pain for parents. You've raised your kids and tried to teach them who Jesus is, and now your kids don't even care about their own souls. They don't care about Jesus. They've walked away from God and his Church, and every time you think of that it crushes your heart once again.

Other couples get married and plan to have a family but are unable to have children. They might say, "Our plan is marriage and a family, so why are we unable to have children?" Perhaps you are a married couple facing infertility, or maybe you are a mother who has gotten pregnant again and again but has lost the baby again and again.

Another kind of insecurity is the life of a single person. Maybe you're just going through life while all your friends have found a spouse and gotten married. You're waiting to find a spouse, because that was your hope and your plan and the thing you counted on, but it just hasn't happened.

In all of these kinds of heartbreak, what do you do? How do you get through the insecurity of these situations when your plans fail? Grieving is necessary. Yet it's really easy not just to respond with grief but to respond with resentment and bitterness. So how do you get through these times of grief?

We are called to recognize that God has not abandoned us here but that he is with us here and will bring us through this. We are called to boldly advance into the shadows of uncertainty.

"I AM THE WAY"

When we don't know the plan, we may question how we can keep walking. We might say, "God, my plan is gone. How do I move forward? I don't know the way." And Jesus has answered that question.

The Gospel of John tells us that St. Thomas asked Jesus that question. When Jesus told his disciples that he was going away, he said to them, "You know the way." Thomas replies, "Lord, we do not know where you are going; how can we know the way?" Then Jesus spoke these words that echo from two thousand years ago to this moment, to your heart. He said, "I am the way" (see John 14:4–6).

If you are thinking, "I don't know where to go from now on," Jesus says, "OK, listen. I am the way." Jesus is saying that he is the plan. Your plans might have been well thought out and good plans. They might have even been holy plans. But in this world of insecurity and uncertainty, Jesus is the plan. Don't put your hope or your confidence in your plan. Put your hope in Jesus. Have confidence in him.

This is how we can choose recognition over resentment. This is how we can get through heartbreak.

God's plan is not that you and I accomplish certain goals or have a certain kind of life. His plan for us is that we each become a certain kind of person. This is why he can say, "I'm the way. Continue to walk with me. I'm the plan. Continue to live with me."

When he is the way and he is the plan, we learn how to become the kind of people who can recognize him at every point in our lives. We can see him in our joys and hear him even in the darkness. We can allow him to love us even in the midst of loss and grief when our plans are shattered. We become the kind of people who can know that he is with us wherever we are. Jesus is the way and the plan, and when we realize this, we become the kind of people who know that we can serve him wherever we are.

RIGHT HERE, RIGHT NOW

My mom never got to be a missionary. She was too busy being a mom. Later on, when we all left the house, she was able to go on some short trips with my dad to do medical missions in Peru and Haiti. But most people would say she never got to be a missionary who did what Jesus described in Matthew 25, feeding the hungry, clothing the naked, and caring for those who were ill and in prison.

But I would tell you this. My mom didn't just go on a couple of mission trips at the end of her life; she spent her life as a missionary. Why? Because she had kids. Babies are born naked, so she spent her life clothing the naked. She gave of herself, her time, her very body feeding the hungry.

She gave drink to the thirsty. You moms know how many times your child comes into your room at night and says, "I'm thirsty." Moms don't say, "You know where the water is, you go get it." No—moms get out of bed. She even visited the imprisoned because when we were grounded, she visited us.

We have these dreams, these plans for where God is going to use us and make us holy. But the place where God makes us holy and gives us a mission is very rarely somewhere else; almost always, is it right here. It is very rarely some other time; almost always, it is right now.

> The place where God gives us a mission and makes us holy is almost always right here and right now.

Now that my mom and dad are empty nesters, my mom can't visit us often or make us meals, but she prays for us. She fasts for us. She can't preach, but she sends us emails all the time about what's true and good that we need to know. Just like your life and my life, it's probably not glamorous, but it's powerful.

You had a plan and I had a plan, and the way you and I are living right now might not be part of the plan we had. The way you and I are called to live right now is probably not glamorous, but it can be powerful.

Where you are right now and where you're going to be led tomorrow is a path through a world of insecurity, but it's not a path we walk alone. We are called to boldly advance into the shadows of uncertainty, to boldly walk through a world of insecurity. It probably won't be your plan, but it will be something better.

REFLECT

What is one time in your life when you had a plan that came to an end and you weren't sure what to do next? What did you do?

Our plans fail, but God's plan never fails. Do you usually surrender to God's plan instead of trying to do it by yourself? If not, how can you practically start accepting God's plan instead of your own?

What are your plans for the near future?

How important do you think it is to look ahead and do your best to make plans? Do you find this easy or do you hesitate to make plans?

Have you, or anyone you've known, ever been convinced of your next step but found that your plan didn't work out the way you thought it would? What are some of the normal conclusions someone would come to when that happened?

Failed plans usually result either in resentment or in recognition that God is in charge. Have you experienced both of these reactions? What does it look like to choose recognition over resentment?

What areas of your life are hardest to surrender to God's plan? How can you place your security in him instead of your own plans?

How can we move forward when we don't know the plan? What does this look like in your life?

PRAY

Sometimes we put so much time and effort into our plans that it can be incredibly painful when they do not pan out the way we had expected. We can feel off-balance and lost when the path we had mapped out for ourselves turns out to be a dead end.

As you enter into prayer, ask the Lord to see your plans clearly and that he might tweak or even completely alter them according to his will. Commit yourself in prayer to accepting with trust wherever God takes you, knowing that any change he makes to *your* plans will be for something better—*his* plan.

For the conclusion of your prayer time, remember that Jesus is the way. He is *your* way. He is your path. He is the entirety of your journey. All plans lead to him. All futures lie in him. Even the times you wander off the path will lead you to him, if you let them. As St. Paul tells us, "All things work for good for those who love God" (Romans 8:28, NAB). If you make your life a continual prayer to the Lord, you will never lose your way.

ACT ///

Surrender your plans to God and ask him to walk through this uncertain world with you. Let him be your security!

REMEMBER

- As we walk through this world that is insecure, we can have enduring faith and hope. In a time of insecurity, we are called to have trust in Jesus' great mercy.

- Life for the Christian is a life spent not at home. Yet we can live powerfully because we have hope that is based on a person, not an outcome. We are called to act even when all seems lost, because our hope is in Jesus.

- As Catholics, we are called to be untroubled by the unknown. We know enough to be courageous in the midst of insecurity and to be confident in the Lord's voice.

- Our plans often fail, but God has a plan that does not fail. In this world of insecurity, Jesus is the plan and the way. He calls us to serve him right here and right now.

NOTES

1   Maria Faustina Kowalska, *Diary: Divine Mercy in My Soul* (Stockbridge, MA: Marian Fathers of the Immaculate Conception, 1987), 9.

2   See Kowalska, 723.

3   Sister Faustina records the Lord's promise of this extraordinary grace in *Diary*, 300, 699, and 1109.

4   Kowalska, 1541.

5   Kowalska, 48.

6   A 1997 poll of 25,000 readers conducted by Britain's Channel 4 and the Waterstone's bookstore chain named *The Lord of the Rings* the number one book of the century, and a 1999 poll of Amazon customers voted it the best book of the millennium.

7   Jim Collins, *Good to Great: Why Some Companies Make the Leap … And Others Don't* (New York: Harper Business, 2001), 83–85.

8   Peter Jackson, *The Lord of the Rings: The Two Towers* (United States: New Line Cinema, 2002).

9   US Bureau of the Census, "2010 American Community Survey."

10   Carl von Clausewitz, *Principles of War* (North Chelmsford, MA: Courier, 2012).

11   von Clausewitz.

12   Learn more about Fr. Walter Ciszek in his books *With God in Russia* (Ignatius, 1997) and *He Leadeth Me* (Image, 2014); see also Louise Perrotta, "The Priest Who Died Three Times," *The Word Among Us*, April/May 2010 issue.

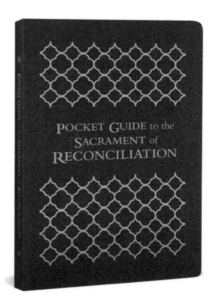